Countries of the World

David Wray

	Country	Size (sq miles)	Population
1	Australia	2,941,283	19,731,984
2	Brazil	3,265,075	182,032,604
3	Canada	3,602,707	32,207,113
4	China	3,600,947	1,286,975,468
5	Dominican Republic	18,700	8,715,602
6	Egypt	386,198	74,718,797
7	France	211,209	60,180,529
8	Germany	137,803	82,398,326
9	Hungary	35,912	10,045,407
10	India	1,147,949	1,049,700,118
11	Ireland	32,375	3,924,140
12	Israel	7,993	6,116,533
13	Japan	146,690	127,214,499
14	Kenya	224,960	31,639,091
15	Lesotho	11,716	1,861,959
16	Mexico	761,830	104,907,991
17	New Zealand	103,736	3,951,307
18	Oman	82,000	2,807,125

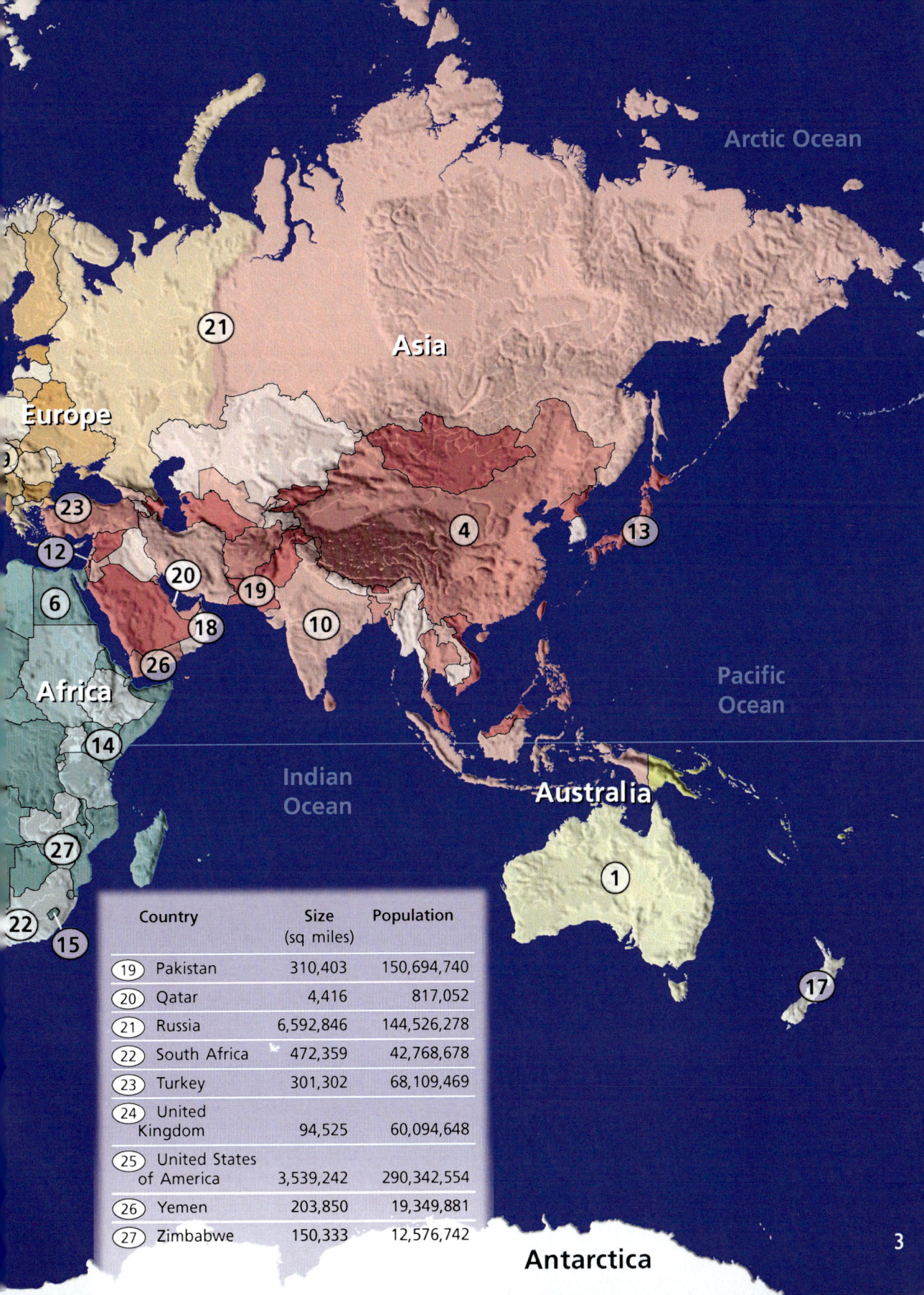

A

Australia

Of all the countries in the world, Australia has the smallest number of people per square mile.

Australian dollar

AUSTRALIA

The Great Barrier Reef stretches for more than 1,350 miles.

Sydney
Canberra
Melbourne
Tasmania

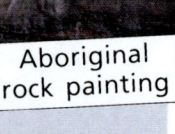
Aboriginal rock painting

Uluru (Ayers Rock) is a sacred site for some Aborigines.

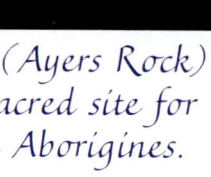

Sydney Opera House is on Sydney Harbor.

A koala

The people of Australia enjoy sports of all kinds. About 6.5 million people, nearly a third of the **population**, are regularly active in sports. Many more are involved in activities such as fishing, walking, boating, riding horses, and fitness programs.

Australians are also enthusiastic sports fans. Crowds of more than 100,000 soccer lovers regularly attend the Australian Football League Grand Final in Melbourne.

Brazil

Brazil is the largest country in South America.

Pele was Brazil's greatest soccer player.

The Amazon **rain forest** supports one-fifth of the world's plants and animals.

The Mardi Gras Carnival in Rio de Janeiro is held for four days every year.

Brazilian real

A boa constrictor

A tropical butterfly

The people of Brazil are great soccer fans, and their country's team has always done well in the World Cup. It first won the Cup in 1958, beating Sweden in the final by five goals to two. Brazil's most famous soccer player, Pele, scored two of the goals.

Brazil won the Cup again in 1962 and again in 1970. Because it was the first country to win the Cup three times, it was given the original trophy.

5

C

Canada

Canada is in North America. It is the second largest country in the world.

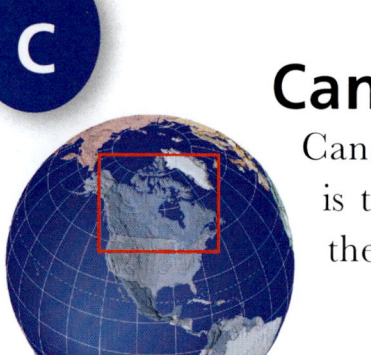

The CN Tower is visited by two million people every year.

Canadian dollar

A moose

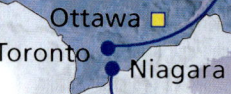

The Rocky Mountains stretch for almost 3,000 miles through Canada and the USA.

The Niagara Falls are on the U.S./Canadian border.

Mounties

The city of Toronto in Canada is home to one of the world's tallest buildings, the 1,150 foot (350 m) high CN Tower. At the top of this tower is the world's highest restaurant, which revolves once every 72 minutes.

Just below the CN Tower is the SkyDome where the Toronto Blue Jays play baseball. The SkyDome was the world's first sports stadium to have a roof that could be pulled back.

China

There are more people in China than in any other country.

The Great Wall of China is so big it is visible from space.

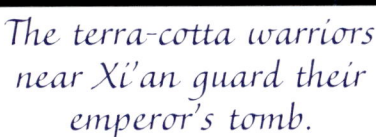

The terra-cotta warriors near Xi'an guard their emperor's tomb.

Hong Kong is the busiest container port in the world.

Chinese food is very popular in other countries. However, most people do not know that there are different types of Chinese food. Eastern Chinese food, from the Shanghai area, is known for its seafood and sugary taste. Western Chinese food, from Szechuan, uses a lot of chili peppers, making it hot and spicy. Southern Cantonese food has sweet and sour combinations. In the north of the country, people eat Pekinese food, which is very rich and filling. Their most famous dish is Peking Duck.

Chinese yuan

Chinese writing

A giant panda

D

Dominican Republic

The Dominican Republic is part of an island in the Caribbean.

Santo Domingo is the oldest city in the "New World" but has a modern industrial port.

Dominican peso

Santo Domingo

DOMINICAN REPUBLIC

The Dominican Republic grows lots of fruit and vegetables.

Plantain trees

Many tourists visit the country for its water sports.

A porcupine fish

In 1492, Christopher Columbus set off from Spain to find the "East Indies," which were islands in the Pacific. Instead, he reached a "New World" that he had not guessed was there. The first place he landed in the Americas was an island we now call the Dominican Republic.

Many people from Spain came to live on this island, and the main language is Spanish.

8

Egypt

Egypt is in north Africa and is famous for its pyramids.

The Nile is the world's longest river.

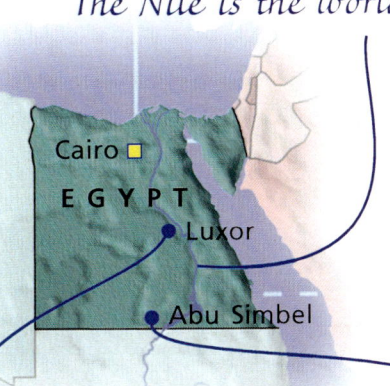

A busy street in Luxor

The Temple of Ramses II in Abu Simbel

Life in Egypt has always been based in the towns and villages along the banks of the Nile River. On each side of the river the land is green and **fertile**, but beyond these narrow strips of land there is nothing but hot, dry desert.

Egyptian farmers use these fertile strips to grow fruit, vegetables, rice, and cotton. The cotton is made into a cloth that is very famous. Sheets are often made of Egyptian cotton.

Egyptian pound

A Nile crocodile

The Great Sphinx in Giza

F

France

France is one of the largest countries in Europe.

The Arc de Triomphe is the largest arch of its kind in the world.

The euro

Eiffel Tower

Cyclists

French chateaux were built as fortresses in medieval times.

France is famous for its food, and food is very important to the people of France. Some of the top chefs in the world have studied at the famous cooking school, Le Cordon Bleu. A meal at a traditional French restaurant will feature crispy breads and rich creamy sauces. France has more than 400 official kinds of cheese and is internationally famous for its amazing desserts.

Grapes for wine are grown in vineyards.

France is also famous for its style and design. Some of the world's greatest works of art, including the "Mona Lisa" by Leonardo da Vinci, are housed in the Louvre Museum in Paris. Many famous clothing designers make Paris their home.

Germany

Germany is the home of the autobahn – the fastest highway system in the world.

The Reichstag is the parliament building in Berlin.

Castles can be seen all along the Rhine valley.

The euro

A holiday market at night

A Volkswagen

A part of the Berlin Wall

The German people take their cars seriously. Germany is one of the top producers of automobiles in the world. It is also home to the speediest drivers. On the autobahn highway system, there are suggested speed limits of 80 miles (130 km) per hour, but many people drive much faster!

Germany is also known for its colorful holiday celebrations. The Christmas tree is a tradition that began in Germany. Oktoberfest, a German harvest celebration, is now a fun event in many other places around the world. All holidays feature rich food and fun.

Hungary

The Danube River flows through the center of Hungary.

The Danube River splits Budapest into two parts – Buda and Pest.

Hungarian forint

Franz Liszt

Traditional dancers

Lake Balaton is the warmest lake in Europe.

Goulash

Hungarians speak a language called Magyar (pronounced Mawdyar), which is very different from other languages in Europe. The language that is closest to Magyar is Finnish, although Finns and Hungarians cannot usually understand each other. The Magyar word for "thank you," for example, is "köszönöm" (kersernerm), but the Finnish word is "kiitos" (keetoss).

Hungarians are very fond of music, and there have been many famous Hungarian musicians, such as the composers Liszt and Bartók.

India

India is the biggest country in southern Asia.

The Taj Mahal is made of marble and precious stones.

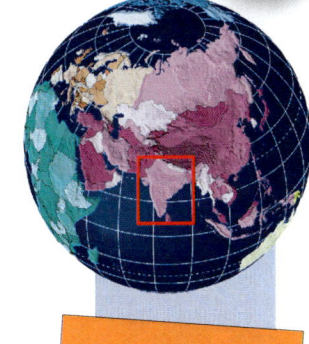

Rickshaws are popular forms of transportation in many Indian cities.

The Ganges River is a holy place. People go there to wash and pray.

A decorated elephant

A snake charmer

Many people claim that the Taj Mahal at Agra is the most beautiful building in the world. It was built by the emperor Jahangir as a memorial to his wife, Mumtaz Mahal, who died after they had been married for 19 years. It took 20,000 workers 20 years to build. It is made of white marble and is surrounded by pools and gardens.

The hot **climate** in India means that people wear light, loose clothes to keep cool. Women often wear saris, which are long pieces of cloth draped like dresses.

I

Ireland

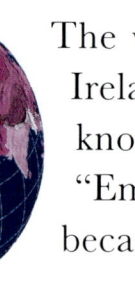

The whole island of Ireland is sometimes known as the "Emerald Isle" because it is so green.

Large crowds attend Gaelic soccer matches.

The euro

A shamrock

Galway Bay is a large bay on the west coast.

A door in Dublin

St. Patrick's Day (March 17) is a national holiday in Ireland. There are parades in the capital city of Dublin and throughout the country.

St. Patrick is the patron saint of Ireland, and, according to the legend, he got rid of all the snakes in the country and gave the Irish their national **symbol**, the shamrock. He lived more than 1,500 years ago.

Kissing the Blarney Stone

Irish people are often said to have the "blarney" (the gift of talking with great skill). People kiss the Blarney Stone to see if it will give them this gift.

14

Israel

Israel is a young country with an ancient history.

Jerusalem is a holy city for many modern-day religions.

Israeli shekel

The Dead Sea is so salty that people who swim in it cannot sink!

ISRAEL
Jerusalem

An olive grove

Israel is a modern-day melting pot of people from many countries and different religions. This small country has made large advances in the sciences, especially where health care is concerned. Many cutting-edge advances in surgery, research, and treatment have been discovered and refined by Israeli doctors and scientists.

Lighting candles at Hanukkah, the Jewish Festival of Lights

J

Japan

Japan is made up of a group of islands in the northern Pacific Ocean.

The bullet train (shinkansen) is the fastest train in the world.

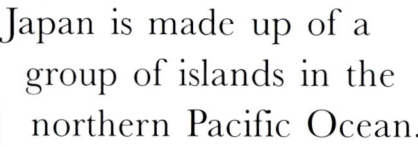

Japanese yen

The beautiful Golden Pavilion at Kyoto is a Buddhist temple.

JAPAN
Kyoto Tokyo

Japanese lanterns

A tea pavilion

Fans

The Japanese are very fond of tea and often drink it in special **ceremonies** called *chaji*. Hot water is poured from a jar called a *mizusashi* on to tea in a bowl (a *chawan*). The bowl is then passed to each guest, who sips the liquid.

Japanese children use pencils and pens to write, but they still learn **calligraphy**, with a brush dipped in ink. At school, children learn *kanji*, which is Japanese writing in Chinese characters.

Kenya

Kenya is a large country in east Africa. It lies on the equator.

A young Maasai herder

Nairobi is a modern, industrial city.

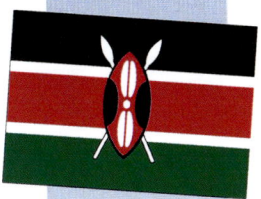

Kenyan shilling

Maasai girl

Tourists on safari

A rhino

Kenya has many wildlife parks. Herds of elephants and other animals live in them. There are many "big cats" such as lions, leopards, and cheetahs. These cats live by hunting the wildebeest, gazelles, and zebras that live in the parks.

Tourists go on **safari** in the parks. Local people act as guides and wildlife wardens to protect the animals. Once, tourists on safari would have shot the animals, but now they only take photographs.

L

Lesotho

Lesotho is a small country that is completely surrounded by South Africa.

*Basotho **herders** in the Drakensberg mountains*

Maseru is the capital of Lesotho.

Basotho costume

Basotho wall hanging

Lesotho (pronounced le-soo-too) is a mountainous kingdom. The whole country is higher than 3,300 feet (1,000 m) above sea level, and some mountains reach up to 10,000 feet (3,000 m). The tourist name for the country is "kingdom in the sky." Lesotho's rough countryside and high mountains have helped the people of Lesotho, the Basotho, to remain **independent**.

Maletsunyane Falls is the highest waterfall in Lesotho.

Basotho herders on the plains of Lesotho wear colorful blankets as they guard their cattle.

18

Mexico

There are 5,800 miles (9,330 km) of coastline in Mexico.

The Temple of the Moon at Teotihuacan is more than 2,000 years old.

Mexican peso

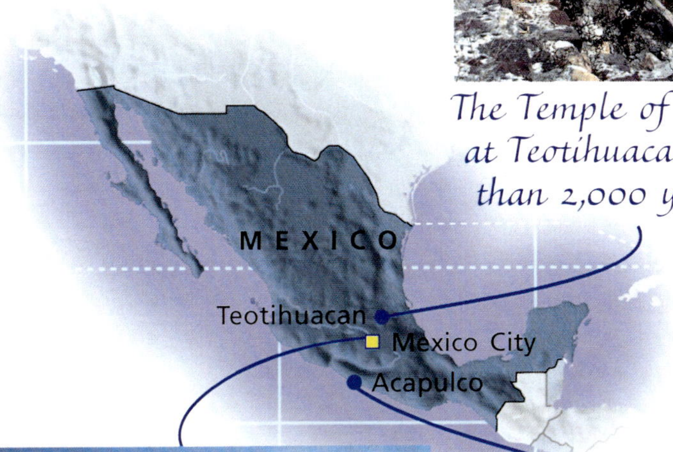

Mayan sculpture

Mexican hats

Mexico City's cathedral was built by the Spanish from 1573 to 1667.

A cliff diver at La Quebrada Cliffs near Acapulco

Many ancient peoples lived in Mexico. The best known are the Mayans and the Aztecs. The Mayans learned to measure time and the movement of the planets. They developed a calendar, which they used for predicting dates that they believed would be lucky or unlucky. Nobody knows quite why the Mayan civilization disappeared.

The Spanish came to Mexico in the 16th century. Today, Spanish is the main language of Mexico.

N

New Zealand

New Zealand is made up of a group of islands in the South Pacific Ocean.

The All Blacks, New Zealand's rugby team

A Maori carving

Thermal springs outside Rotorua

A kiwi

The Mount Cook region has some beautiful **glaciers**.

People from New Zealand are often given the nickname "Kiwis." This is because of a bird called a kiwi that is found nowhere else in the world. Kiwis only come out at night. During the day they sleep in burrows in the ground. They have long beaks and feathers that look like hair.

The original inhabitants of New Zealand were the Maoris, who sailed there from other islands in the Pacific Ocean. European settlers began to arrive in New Zealand during the 19th century.

Oman

Oman is a small country east of Saudi Arabia, at the entrance to the Persian Gulf.

Old stone forts are found in many villages.

There are big markets called souks.

A Bedouin camp at Wahiba Sands

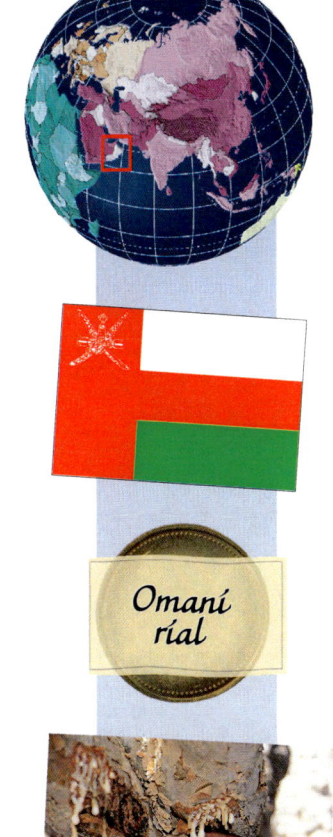
Frankincense resin

Dates

Oman has been important for centuries because of the frankincense trees that grow around the city of Salalah. Frankincense was one of the most precious materials in the ancient world. It was supposed to have healing powers.

Frankincense trees are thorny, but when an area of their bark is cut, white resin oozes out. These drops are left on the tree to harden and are then collected. Frankincense is still sold in the markets, although most is now used to make perfumes.

P

Pakistan

Pakistan is a large country to the northwest of India, through which flows the great Indus River.

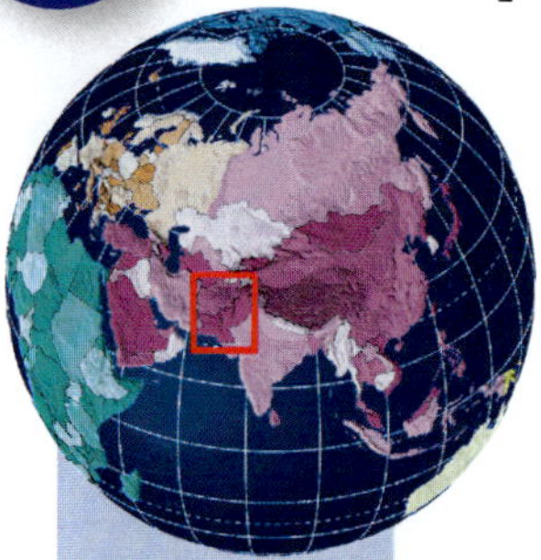

The famous Khyber Pass connects Pakistan with Afghanistan.

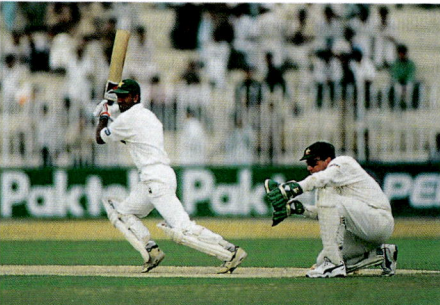

Pakistan has one of the best cricket teams in the world.

A Muslim holy man

Up to 10,000 people gather at Badshahi mosque in Lahore on special days.

A decorated bus

Pakistan is the home of one of the earliest civilizations on Earth, the great Indus Valley civilization, which lay at the heart of several ancient empires. It has spectacular countryside with enormous fertile plains surrounded by some of the highest mountains in the world.

Mountain ranges such as the Karakoram and the Hindu Kush attract mountaineers from around the world.

22

Qatar

Qatar is a very small country in the Middle East that has the world's largest-known reserves of natural gas.

Bedouin use camels to travel across the desert.

An oil rig at sea

Fishermen use these traditional sailing boats called dhows.

An Arabian oryx

Bedouin weaving

Qatari riyal

The people of Qatar were originally Bedouin, who traveled from place to place rather than living in a house. Although most Qataris are no longer **nomadic** in this way, they still produce many Bedouin things, such as tents, rugs, cushions, and saddlebags. These are woven from the wool of sheep, goats, and camels, using simple tools made from wood or gazelle horn.

Traditional Qatari dress is rich with gold or silver embroidery. Women wear veils and often a black mask, called *al-battoulah*, which covers all of their face except the eyes, nose, and mouth. Qatari men wear a *thobe*, which is a long, white shirt over loose trousers.

23

R

Russia

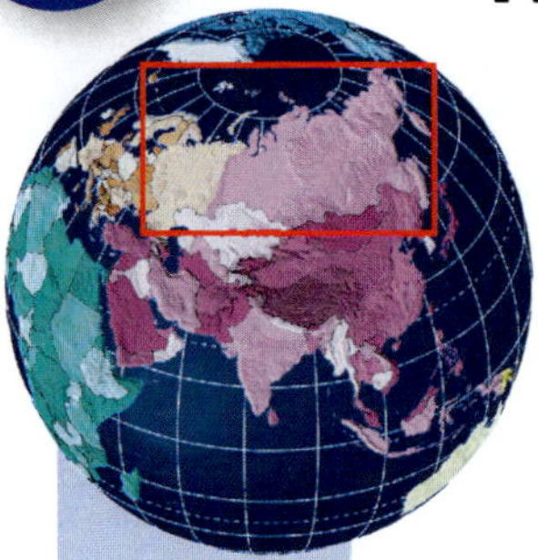

Russia is the world's largest country and crosses two **continents**, Europe and Asia.

Russian winters bring ice, snow, and freezing temperatures.

Russian ruble

Russian hat

Russian eggs

Inside the famous Hermitage Museum in St. Petersburg

The colorful St. Basil's cathedral is in Red Square, Moscow.

Russia was the largest country in what used to be called the Soviet Union. Today, many of the other countries of the Soviet Union, such as Ukraine and Georgia, are independent countries.

In Siberia, the Asian part of Russia, is Lake Baikal, which contains almost one-quarter of all the fresh water on Earth. At 5,300 feet (1,620 m) deep, it is the deepest lake in the world.

South Africa

The country of South Africa is at the southern end of the continent of Africa.

Table Mountain towers over Cape Town.

This woman is wearing traditional Ndebele dress.

South African rand

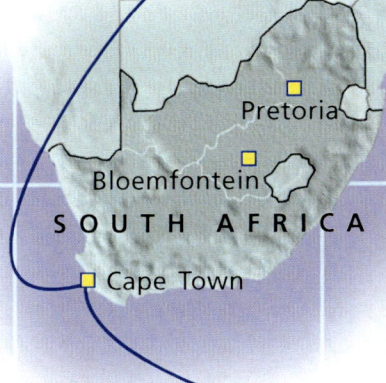

The Waterfront in Cape Town

Nelson Mandela

A King Protea flower

South Africa's most famous person is Nelson Mandela. For nearly 50 years he fought against the apartheid system (the forced separation of white and black people). In 1964, he was sentenced to life in prison, but even from prison he urged people to carry on the struggle against apartheid.

After 27 years in prison, Nelson Mandela was freed. Less than five years after his release, he was awarded the Nobel Peace Prize and became president of his country.

25

T

Turkey

Turkey spans two **continents**, Europe and Asia.

The Blue Mosque in Istanbul has six minarets.

Turkish lira

Shish kebab

Archeologists have found nine cities at Troy, each built on top of another.

Until 1923, the capital of Turkey was Istanbul. The city is built on both sides of the Bosphorus Strait, which separates Europe from Asia. Istanbul was built in 600 BC and was known first as Byzantium, then Constantinople before it became Istanbul in 1453. Today, the capital of Turkey is Ankara.

Turkish carpet

At the Grand Bazaar in Istanbul you can buy leather, gold, and pottery.

United Kingdom

The United Kingdom, or UK, is made up of England, Scotland, Wales, and Northern Ireland.

People say that the Giant's Causeway in Northern Ireland was built as a trail for giants.

British pound sterling

Caernarfon Castle in Wales was built 700 years ago.

The London Eye on the River Thames gives fantastic views of London.

Big Ben

A Scottish soccer fan

In the UK, in addition to English, some people also speak two Celtic languages (Gaelic in Scotland and Ireland, and Welsh in Wales). The Celts were some of the first people to live in the British Isles. The Romans, Saxons, Vikings, and Normans later invaded parts of the UK.

Soccer is the most popular sport in the UK, and there is always great excitement when the top teams play each other.

27

U

United States of America

The United States of America stretches from the Atlantic and out into the Pacific Ocean.

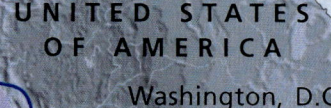

Death Valley in California is the hottest place in the USA.

The Golden Gate Bridge in San Francisco is one of the world's longest suspension bridges.

The White House

Statue of Liberty

The original inhabitants of North America are called Native Americans. There were many different Native American groups in North America, each with its own language and customs. The main groups were the Northwest, Intermountain, Southwest, Plains, and Woodland Indians. The Plains people, such as the Sioux and Cheyenne, lived in tepees and hunted buffalo, but the people of the Northwest lived in wooden cabins and ate salmon and other fish.

Disney World in Florida is one of the USA's most famous attractions.

Today, the United States is home to many different people and customs from other countries.

28

Yemen

Much of Yemen is a very harsh desert, including most of the land along the southern coast.

The Great Mosque at San'a was one of the first mosques to be built in Yemen.

These men are selling gourds to be used as water carriers.

Most of the time this flooded wadi (riverbed) is dry.

Men chewing qat leaves

Yemeni woman

Because most of Yemen is desert, few things grow. Because it is so dry, there are very few animals. Along the west coast, however, there is a great deal of fertile land, and rain falls heavily there for about two months of the year. Farmers grow coffee, spices, and tropical fruit.

Rather than meeting at a restaurant, Yemenis will gather together in the afternoon to chew leaves. They find that chewing the leaves of the *qat* plant is relaxing. A lot of business is done at these afternoon parties.

Z

Zimbabwe

Zimbabwe has no coastline, for it is completely surrounded by other countries.

You can hear the roar of Victoria Falls up to 25 miles (40 km) away.

Much of Zimbabwe is grassland, like the Hwange National Park.

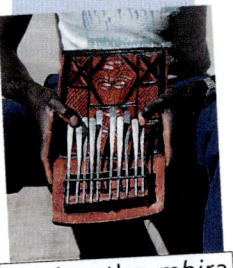

Playing the *mbira*

Cheetah

The ruins of Great Zimbabwe, an ancient fortress, can be seen near Masvingo.

The *mbira* is a popular musical instrument in Zimbabwe. It is a set of metal keys that produce different tones when they are hit. The keys are mounted on a wooden board on the front of which is a metal plate with a row of snail shells. The shells buzz as the *mbira* is played. This buzzing is an important part of the music. Nowadays, bottle tops are often used instead of snail shells.

Zimbabwe's biggest and best-known tourist attraction is the Victoria Falls. At the falls, the Zambezi River, which is more than a mile wide, plunges into a **chasm** 350 feet (106 m) deep.

30

Glossary

calligraphy – the art of beautiful handwriting

ceremony – actions, words, and music performed for a special occasion

chasm – a deep crack in the surface of the Earth

climate – the usual weather in a particular area

continent – one of the Earth's seven large landmasses

cricket – a sport that is similar to baseball, that is played with two teams, a ball, and a wide, flat bat

fertile – able to grow plants or crops

glacier – a huge, slow-moving mass of ice

herder – someone who looks after large groups of animals

independent – not controlled by other people or governments

nomadic – moving from one place to another rather than staying in one place

population – the people who live in a particular place

rain forest – a thick tropical forest in an area that receives a great deal of rain

safari – a journey to see large wild animals

symbol – something that represents something else

thermal springs – hot streams or pools of water that rise up from underground

Index

Aborigines	4	glaciers	20	ports	7, 8
Aztecs	19	herders	17, 18	rain forest	5
Bedouin	21, 23	lakes	12, 24	rivers	9, 12, 13, 22, 27, 29, 30
Carnival	5	languages	8, 12, 19, 27, 28		
castles	10, 11, 27	Maasai	17	safari	17
cathedrals	19, 24	Maoris	20	sports	4, 5, 6, 8, 10, 14, 20, 22, 27
clothes	10, 12, 13, 18, 23, 24, 25	markets	11, 21, 26		
		Mayans	19	temples	9, 16, 19
desert	9, 23, 29	mosques	22, 26, 29	transportation	11, 13, 16, 22
drink	16	mountains	6, 18, 20, 22, 25		
farming	9, 29	music	12, 30	waterfalls	6, 18, 30
food	7, 8, 9, 10, 11, 12, 26	Native Americans	28	writing	7, 16

31

© 2004 **Pacific Learning**
© 2001 Written by **David Wray**
Photography: Allsport: p. 22 (center); Christine Osborne Pictures: pp. 21 (top), (center left), (bottom), (top right), 22 (top), (right), 23 (left), (center), (right), (bottom right), 29 (center); Stephanie Colasanti: pp. 10 (bottom right), 15 (left); Collections/Image Ireland/Mark O'Sullivan: p. 14 (top); Corel: pp. 4 (all), 5 (left), (right), (bottom right), 6 (all), 7 (all), 8 (top left), (left), (bottom left), (right), 9 (top), (center), (right), (bottom right), 10 (center), (top right), (top left), (left), 11 (top), (left), (bottom right), 13 (top), (center), (right), 14 (left), 15 (top), (right), 16 (all), 17 (top), (right), (bottom right), 19 (all), 20 (top), 21 (bottom right), 22 (center left), 24 (top), (center), (right), (bottom left), 25 (bottom center), (center right), 26 (top), (left), 27 (center), (center right), (left), 28 (all), 29 (bottom right), 30 (bottom left); OUP: pp. 18 (bottom left), 26 (bottom left); Robert Harding: pp. 9 (bottom left), 12 (top), (bottom right), 14 (center), (right), 17 (left), 18 (top), 29 (top); Robert Harding/E. Simanor: p. 15 (center bottom); Robert Harding/Camerapix/Mohamed Amin: pp. 17 (center), 20 (bottom left); Robert Harding/Alain Avrard; p. 22 (left); Robert Harding/Ken Wilson: p. 26 (center left); Hungarian Tourist Office: p. 12 (center); Hutchison Library/Jeremy Horner: p. 8 (top right); Hutchison Library/Liba Taylor: p. 18 (center); Hutchison Library/Andzey Zvoznikov: p. 24 (left); Hutchison Library/John Hatt p. 26 (right); Images of Africa/David Keith Jones: p. 30 (top); Lebrecht Collection/Joanne Harris: p. 12 (top left); Panos Pictures/Rui Vieira: p. 18 (left); Panos Pictures/N. Cooper: p. 18 (right); Panos Pictures/Giacomo Pirozzi: p. 29 (left); Panos Pictures/Steve Thomas: p. 30 (bottom right); Panos Pictures/David Reed: p. 30 (top left); Photofusion/Ray Roberts: p. 27 (top); Photofusion/Graham Burns: p. 27 (bottom right); Popperfoto: pp. 5 (top), 20 (right); South American Pictures/Tony Morrison: p. 5 (center bottom); Still Pictures/Max Milligan: p. 30 (center); Travel Ink/Simon Reddy: p. 12 (bottom left); Travel Ink/Julian Looder: p. 29 (right); Tony O'Keefe: pp. 20 (center), (left), 25 (top left), (bottom right); Tony Stone Images/Siegfried Layda: p. 11 (bottom left); Tony Stone/Lorne Resnick: p. 23 (top); Volkswagen Press & PR p. 11 (right); Chrispin Zeeman: pp. 13 (left), (bottom right), 25 (top right).
Front cover photograph by Corel.
All maps and globes based on maps by **Geoatlas**
U.S. edit by **Rebecca McEwen**

All rights reserved. No part of this publication may be reproduced or transmitted in any form or by any means, electronic or mechanical, including photocopying, recording, taping, or any information storage and retrieval system, without permission in writing from the publisher.

This Americanized Edition of *Countries of the World,* originally published in England in 2001, is published by arrangement with Oxford University Press.

Published by
Pacific Learning
P.O. Box 2723
Huntington Beach, CA 92647-0723
www.pacificlearning.com

ISBN: 978-1-59055-410-4
PL-7422

Printed in USA